THE CITY LIBRARY
SPRINGFIELD, (MA) CITY LIBRARY

DISCARDED BY
THE CITY LIBRARY

EMILY'S
PLACE FOR
CHILDREN

This Item Is A Gift
By Generous Donors to
The Springfield Library Foundation

# My First Book of Airplanes

## ALL ABOUT FLYING MACHINES FOR KIDS

KRISTINA A. HOLZWEISS, MSLIS, MA

ROCKRIDGE PRESS

In memory of my father, Charles P. Uihlein

Copyright © 2022 by Rockridge Press

All rights reserved. No part of this publication may be reproduced, stored in a retrieval system, or transmitted in any form or by any means, electronic, mechanical, photocopying, recording, scanning, or otherwise without the prior written permission of the Publisher. Requests to the Publisher for permission should be addressed to the Permissions Department, Rockridge Press, 1955 Broadway, Suite 400, Oakland, CA 94612.

First Rockridge Press edition 2022

Rockridge Press and the Rockridge Press logo are trademarks or registered trademarks of Callisto Media Inc. and/or its affiliates in the United States and other countries and may not be used without written permission.

For general information on our other products and services, please contact our Customer Care Department within the United States at (866) 744-2665, or outside the United States at (510) 253-0500.

Hardcover ISBN: 979-8-88608-916-5
Paperback ISBN: 978-1-68539-563-6
eBook ISBN: 978-1-68539-797-5

Manufactured in the United States of America

Series Designer: Sean Doyle
Interior and Cover Designer: Keirsten Geise
Art Producer: Melissa Malinowsky
Editor: Laura Bryn Sisson
Production Editor: Cassie Gitkin
Production Manager: David Zapanta

Photo credits: iStock cover, and pp. 3, 32; Shutterstock, pp. 4, 7, 12, 27, 41, 43, 47, 48, 55; Public Domain Sourced/Access Rights From The History Collection/Alamy Stock Photo, p. IV; Stephan Rathke/Alamy Stock Photo, p. 8; James Schwabel/Alamy Stock Photo, p. 11; Pictorial Press Ltd/Alamy Stock Photo, p. 14; Ivan Cholakov/Alamy Stock Photo, p. 16; Science History Images/Alamy Stock Photo, p. 19; Aviation History Collection/Alamy Stock Photo, p. 20; GL Archive/Alamy Stock Photo, p. 23; Pictorial Press Ltd/Alamy Stock Photo, p. 24; Aviation History Collection/Alamy Stock Photo, p. 28; SuperStock/Alamy Stock Photo, p. 31; US Air Force Photo/Alamy Stock Photo, p. 35; EThamPhoto/Alamy Stock Photo, p. 36; Anthony Kay/Flight/Alamy Stock Photo, pp. 38-39; RGB Ventures/SuperStock/Alamy Stock Photo, p. 42; Zechina/Alamy Stock Photo, p. 44; Peter de Clercq/Alamy Stock Photo, pp. 50-51; SuperStock/Alamy Stock Photo, p. 52; REUTERS/Alamy Stock Photo, p. 57; Konstantin Yuganov/Alamy Stock Photo, p. 58

10 9 8 7 6 5 4 3 2 1 0

This book belongs to:

_____

Drawing of a helicopter imagined by Leonardo da Vinci

# Prepare for Liftoff!

For thousands of years, people all over the world have dreamed about flying. Ancient Greeks told a **myth** about a man named Daedalus who made **wings** from wax and feathers. Kites were first invented in China to help armies. Italian artist and engineer Leonardo da Vinci drew a **glider**, a helicopter, and a "flying machine."

Today, we can travel by air over short and long distances using flying machines from single-person gliders to jumbo jets. **Airplanes** can transport **cargo** over the ocean faster than ships. Because of what we have learned about flying, we can even travel into space! Let's learn more about airplanes and other **aircraft**.

*Klaus Ohlmann from Germany has held the record for flying the farthest distance in a glider (1,869 miles)!*

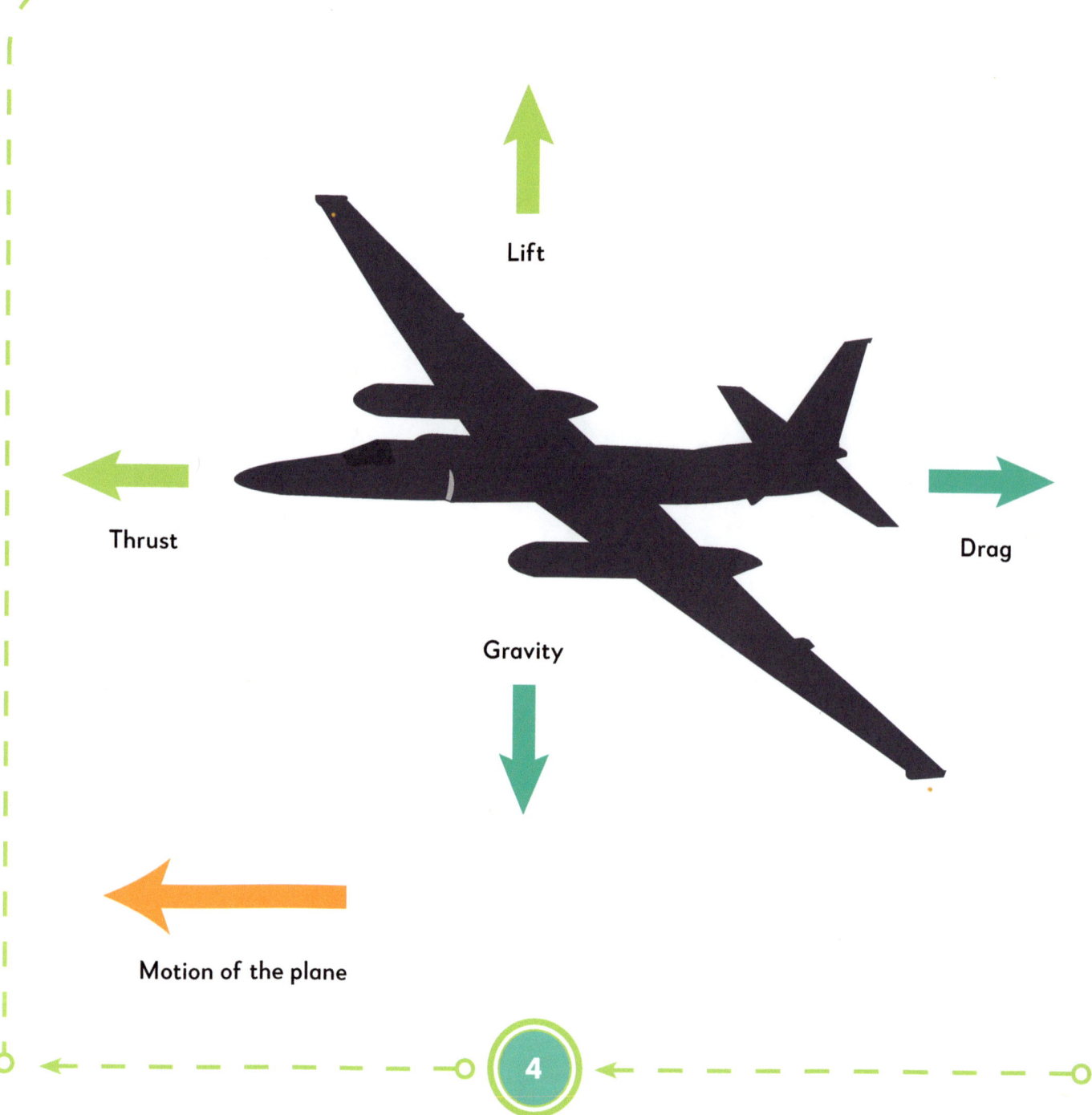

# How Airplanes Work

Airplanes fly because they balance four different forces: **gravity**, **lift**, **thrust**, and **drag**. Gravity is the force between two objects. It pulls us down to Earth so we don't float away. When an airplane flies, it needs to push through the air. Drag is the air's force that slows down the airplane.

The powerful **engine** thrusts the airplane through the air. Wings help airplanes fly with a force called lift. Air moves quickly over specially-shaped wings so the force on top is less than underneath. A pointy airplane nose helps to cut through the air. **Tailfins** in the back help keep the airplane level.

*Early airplanes were made of wood and fabric. Today, many are made of aluminum and titanium.*

A pilot and copilot sitting in a cockpit

## Who's Who

The **pilot** and **copilot** take turns taking off, flying, and landing airplanes. The copilot also takes over if there is an emergency. **Flight attendants** serve the **passengers** on board. From the airport tower, the **air traffic controllers** watch the radar to make sure that the airplanes are safe.

# Types of Aircraft

There are many different types of aircraft. Some airplanes take people on business trips or vacations. Others transport cargo supplies and products for people to buy. **Seaplanes** can land on water. **Military** aircraft keep us safe. We can explore space and the world around us with aircraft.

Space shuttles use rocket engines.

Powered aircraft have engines. They use different engines depending on how big they are. **Piston engines** spin propellers. **Jet engines** are more powerful and are used in large aircraft. **Rocket engines** push aircraft through Earth's atmosphere.

Giffard Dirigible

# Dreaming of Flying

In 1783, two people flew in a hot-air balloon made of silk and paper for 5.5 miles. Then Jacques Charles and Marie-Noël Robert traveled 27 miles in a hydrogen gas balloon. In 1852, the Giffard Dirigible was the first aircraft that was powered and could be guided. **Dirigible** means "can be steered."

*The first-ever hot-air balloon passengers were a rooster, a duck, and a sheep.*

*The* Spirit of Goodyear *blimp holds the world record for the longest continually operated airship, flying from 2000 to 2014.*

# Airships

Unique airships called dirigibles, Zeppelins, and **blimps** use gases lighter than air to fly. They were the most common form of air transportation until faster airplanes were invented and became popular. Today, photographers take pictures and record videos at sports events and concerts from blimps. Companies also advertise on blimps.

# The First Airplane

On December 17, 1903, brothers Wilbur and Orville Wright achieved the first controlled flight of a heavier-than-air powered airplane. Wilbur flew their airplane for 59 seconds over a distance of 852 feet at Kitty Hawk, North Carolina. Their airplane had a **rudder** and **angled wings** like a bird.

The Wright brothers testing their airplane

Two Douglas World Cruiser biplanes made the first flight around the world in 1924. The trip lasted 175 days across 27,000 miles. Together they landed in 22 different countries.

# Biplanes

**Biplanes** have two sets of wings ("bi" means two). One set is attached to the body or **fuselage** of the airplane, and the other set sits above the body. Most early airplanes were biplanes. They were stiff and strong, but they were not very fast. They had open **cockpits**, and pilots wore warm clothes, helmets, and goggles.

**Douglas World Cruiser**
**Crew:** 2
**Length:** 35 feet, 6 inches
**Height:** 13 feet, 7 inches
**Wingspan:** 50 feet
**Maximum Speed:** 103 miles per hour

Biplane wings are short so they are easy to **maneuver**. Biplanes were mostly used between 1914 and 1918. After 1939, biplanes were used for **crop dusting** and stunt flying. Stunt pilot Bessie Coleman was the first African American woman and the first Native American to earn a pilot's license.

Pilot Bessie Coleman

Charles Lindberg and the *Spirit of St. Louis*.

# Monoplanes

When engines became more powerful around 1939, **monoplanes** with one set of wings were built ("mono" means one). Large monoplane wings can be attached under, on the mid sides, or on top of the fuselage. Monoplanes fly faster than biplanes but don't maneuver as well. Modern airplanes are monoplanes.

*Spirit of St. Louis*
**Crew:** 1
**Length:** 27 feet, 8 inches
**Height:** 9 feet, 8 inches
**Wingspan:** 46 feet
**Maximum Speed:** 133 miles per hour

In 1927, Charles Lindbergh made the first **solo** nonstop flight in the *Spirit of St. Louis* monoplane over the Atlantic Ocean from Long Island, New York, to Paris, France, in 33 hours. Amelia Earhart was the first woman to fly solo from New York to Paris in her Lockheed Vega 5B in 1932.

In 1935, Amelia Earhart became the first person to fly solo from Hawaii to California. She crossed 2,400 miles in 18 hours.

The Gee Bee R-1, piloted by Jimmy Doolittle, set a world landplane speed record of 296 miles per hour when he won the Thompson Trophy race.

# Gee Bee Racers

Gee Bee Super Sportster Racers (models Z, R-1, and R-2) were designed by Granville Brothers Aircraft to compete in the 1932 Thompson Trophy race. These monoplanes looked strange with their wide bodies, low wings, and cockpit located at the back of the airplane. Only experienced pilots could fly these very fast airplanes.

**Gee Bee Super Sportster R-1**
**Crew:** 1
**Length:** 17 feet, 8 inches
**Height:** 8 feet, 2 inches
**Wingspan:** 75 feet
**Maximum Speed:** 296 miles per hour

# Flying Boats

Flying boat airplanes have boat-like **hulls** that help them float on water. Without landing gear for runways, flying boats can land and take off from the water while carrying passengers and heavy cargo. The Spruce Goose, a flying boat built by Howard Hughes, is the largest wooden airplane ever made. But it only flew for thirty seconds.

**"Spruce Goose" Hughes Aircraft H-R Hercules**
**Crew:** 4
**Length:** 218 feet, 8 inches
**Height:** 79 feet, 4 inches
**Wingspan:** 320 feet, 11 inches
**Maximum Speed:** 135 miles per hour

KLM Royal Dutch Airlines, founded in 1919, is the oldest airline in the world still using its original name.

# First Modern Airliners

An **airliner** transports passengers and cargo. Passengers can fly nonstop on **commercial** flights for as short as less than a minute between two islands in Scotland, to almost 19 hours from New York to Singapore. The Boeing 247, Douglas DC2, and Douglas DC3 were some of the first modern passenger airplanes and carried between 10 and 28 passengers at a time.

# X-Planes

X-planes are aircraft designed to test new technologies and **aerodynamics**. They are used mainly at Edwards Air Force Base. X-planes have been designed to test missiles, **vertical** takeoff and landing, and **unmanned** flight. Most X-planes are sample models, or **prototypes**, and many have broken range, speed, and altitude records.

In 1948, the Bell X-1, piloted by United States Air Force officer Chuck Yeager, was the first aircraft to fly faster than the speed of sound—957 miles per hour.

Jet engine of an aircraft

# Jets

Unlike airplanes powered by propellers, jets move with jet engines. The engine burns fuel with air that enters through an **intake** and is then **compressed** by a fan. Jets are powered by the high-energy gas stream released from the engine **exhaust**. Commercial, private, and military jets are faster and can fly higher than regular airplanes.

**Concorde**
**Crew:** 3
**Length:** 202 feet, 4 inches
**Height:** 40 feet
**Wingspan:** 84 feet
**Maximum Speed:** 1,354 miles per hour

*The Concorde was a jet that allowed passengers to travel between London and New York in about three hours.*

# Jumbo Jets

During the 1960s, travel by airplane became very popular. So companies began making bigger, wider, more powerful jumbo jets. The first jumbo jet, the Boeing 747, could fly more than 350 people from New York to London. The upper level could be a lounge for people who paid extra for first class.

**Space Shuttle *Atlantis* riding on a Boeing 747**

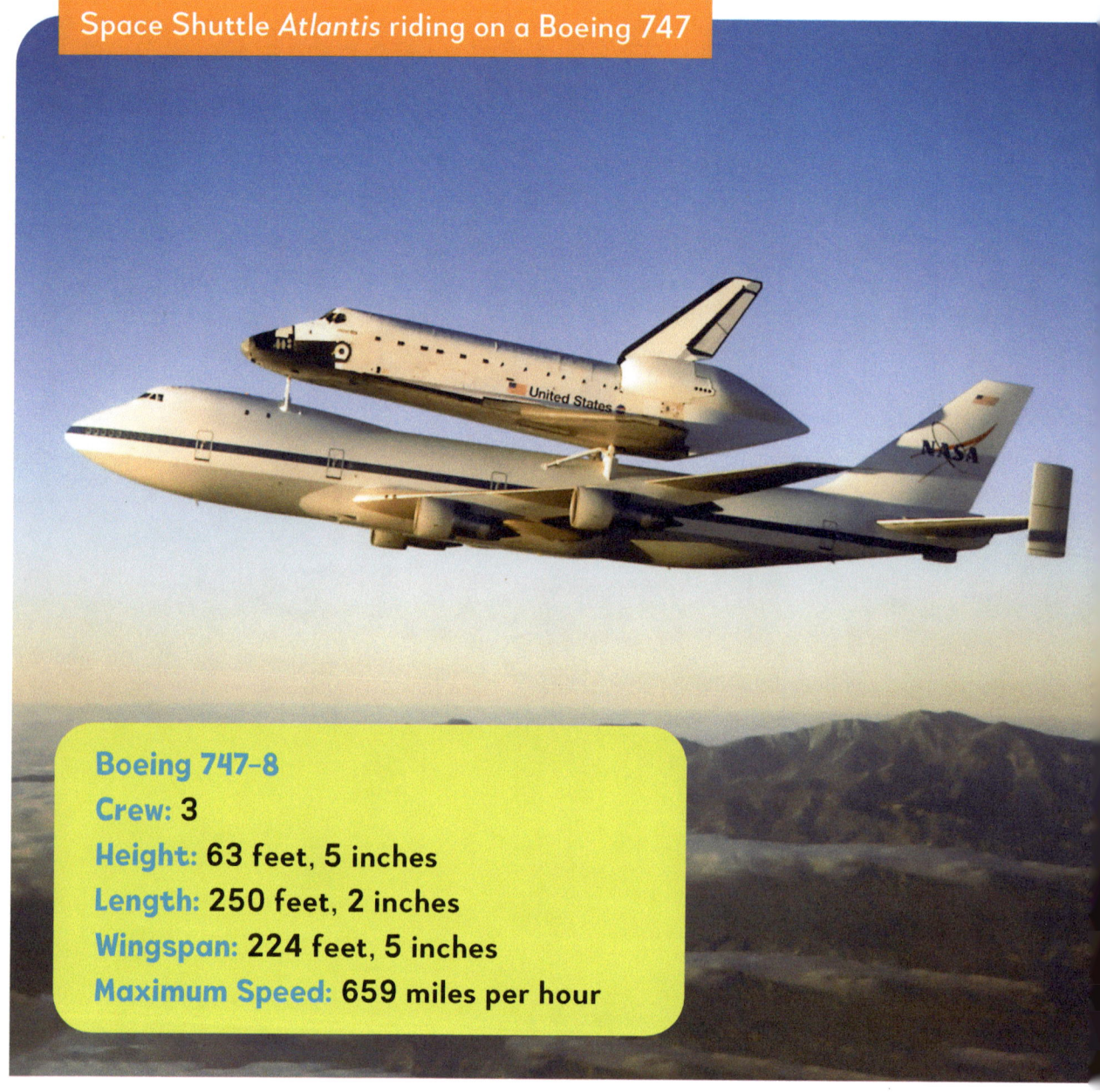

**Boeing 747-8**
**Crew:** 3
**Height:** 63 feet, 5 inches
**Length:** 250 feet, 2 inches
**Wingspan:** 224 feet, 5 inches
**Maximum Speed:** 659 miles per hour

*Air Force One,* two Boeing 747-200B jumbo jets
**Crew:** 3
**Length:** 231 feet, 10 inches
**Height:** 63 feet, 5 inches
**Wingspan:** 195 feet, 8 inches
**Maximum Speed:** 600 miles per hour

# Private Jets

Private jets are owned by companies or wealthy people who can afford them, like businesspeople, celebrities, athletes, and royalty. Passengers on private jets can fly alone or with anyone they invite and have more room to be comfortable. Since they hire their flight crew, passengers can travel whenever and wherever they choose to.

# Stunt Flying

Since the beginning of **aviation**, pilots have amazed audiences with stunt flying. Stunt pilots are trained to fly **aerobatics** ("aerial" + "acrobatics") like spins, loop-the-loops, barrel rolls, and nose dives. **Aerialists** walk across airplane wings and jump from parachutes. Some pilots can fly their jets as close as 18 inches apart!

Air ambulance

# Aircraft That Help Us

Airplanes can be used in many different ways. Cargo planes transport goods from place to place. Some passenger airplanes also carry mail. **Air ambulances** are planes that have special equipment to transport injured or sick people in emergencies.

Water scooper dumping water

Crop dusters help farmers spread pesticides to control insects and weeds. **Top dressers** spread **fertilizer** to help plants grow. Air tankers spread fire retardant to help put out fires. **Water scoopers** fly very quickly and low so they can scoop up water from lakes to dump onto fires.

*Did you know that you don't need a license to fly an ultralight glider? Even kids are allowed to fly ultralights on their own!*

# Ultralight Gliders

In an ultralight glider, the pilot's seat hangs below the wing. These gliders are powered by propellers, and the pilot uses weight-shift to steer. This means they lean the weight of their body to control the plane. Ultralight gliders only carry the pilot and sometimes one other passenger. Other types of gliders are hang gliders, sailplanes, and even the space shuttle!

# Space Planes

Space planes use rocket engines. These engines don't need oxygen from the atmosphere to burn fuel like jet engines do. This allows space planes to fly higher than jet engines can, into outer space. In the future, space planes might help scientists learn more about space. Space planes even carry passengers who just want to ride for fun.

**SpaceShipTwo**
**Crew:** 2
**Length:** 60 feet
**Height:** 18 feet
**Wingspan:** 27 feet
**Maximum Speed:** 2,500 miles per hour

# Solar Airplanes

**Solar-powered** airplanes get energy from the sun's rays and change it into **electricity** using panels on the wings. At night or when it is cloudy, solar-powered airplanes are powered by electricity from batteries. Solar-powered airplanes are cleaner than other airplanes because they don't burn fuel. Using solar energy instead of fuel is less harmful to the Earth.

*The Solar Impulse 2 was the first solar-powered airplane to fly around the world.*

# Airplanes and You

From dreaming we could fly to traveling to outer space, we have designed so many amazing aircraft around the world. In the future, we will invent even faster and higher ways to fly that are cleaner for the environment. Where would you like to fly someday?

# GLOSSARY

**AERIALISTS:** People who perform dangerous stunts on flying airplanes

**AEROBATICS:** Acrobatics performed in the air

**AERODYNAMICS:** Study of how air moves

**AIR AMBULANCES:** Aircraft with special equipment that transport injured or sick people in emergencies

**AIRCRAFT:** A machine that can fly

**AIRLINER:** An airplane that transports passengers or cargo

**AIRPLANES:** Powered aircraft that have fixed wings and are heavier than air

**AIR TRAFFIC CONTROLLERS:** People who direct airplanes on the ground and in the air

**ANGLED WINGS:** Wings that aren't level; turned upward or downward

**AVIATION:** Using aircraft

**BIPLANES:** Airplanes with two sets of wings

**BLIMPS:** Powered, steerable aircraft that float because they are inflated with a gas lighter than air

**CARGO:** Goods that are transported

**COCKPIT:** Area at the front of the airplane where the pilot and copilot sit

**COMMERCIAL:** Used for making money

**COMPRESSED:** Squeezed or pressed together

**COPILOT:** The pilot's assistant

**CROP DUSTING:** Spraying chemicals on plants to keep pests from eating them

**DIRIGIBLE:** A steerable craft lighter than air

**DRAG:** Air's force that slows down the airplane

**ELECTRICITY:** Energy that can build up in one place or flow from one place to another

**ENGINE:** A machine that uses energy from fuel or electricity to do work

**EXHAUST:** Gas that comes out of the engine

**FERTILIZER:** Makes plants grow quicker, taller, and bigger

**FLIGHT ATTENDANTS:** People who serve and help passengers on an aircraft

**FUSELAGE:** Body of an airplane

**GLIDERS:** Aircraft that fly through the air without motors

**GRAVITY:** Force between two objects

**HULL:** Part of a boat that rides in and on top of the water

**INTAKE:** The place where liquid or air is taken into something

**JET ENGINES:** Engines that make something move when hot air and gas are released from the back

**LIFT:** The upward force that helps an airplane fly

**MILITARY:** Group of people who defend their country

**MONOPLANES:** Airplanes with only one set of wings

**MYTH:** A story that explains something, usually in nature

**PASSENGERS:** People traveling in a vehicle

**PILOT:** A person who takes off, flies, and lands the airplane

**PISTON ENGINES:** Engines that use a cylinder that slides in a tube

**PROTOTYPE:** A first model of an invention

**ROCKET ENGINES:** Engines that make something move upward when hot air and gas are released from the back; must carry their oxygen supply

**RUDDER:** A part of an airplane that helps steer it

**SEAPLANES:** Airplanes that can land on water

**SOLAR-POWERED:** Gets energy from the sun for fuel

**SOLO:** Alone

**TAILFINS:** Parts at the back of the airplane that keep it level

**THRUST:** Force that moves an aircraft through the air

**TOP DRESSERS:** Airplanes that spray fertilizer on crops

**UNMANNED:** Moving on its own without a pilot or crew

**VERTICAL:** In an up and down direction

**WATER SCOOPERS:** Airplanes that gather water from lakes and dump it on fires

**WINGS:** Part of an aircraft that helps it lift

## ABOUT THE AUTHOR

 **Kristina A. Holzweiss** is the 2015 *School Library Journal* School Librarian of the Year, a National School Board "20 to Watch" emerging education technology leader in 2016 and 2017, and a 2018 *Library Journal* Mover & Shaker. She is a librarian, educator, author, international presenter, library advocate, and keynote speaker. Kristina is the founder of SLIME (Students of Long Island Maker Expo) and a founding member of the Nation of Makers. Kristina enjoys speaking to librarians, educators, and students.

Follow Kristina on Twitter at @lieberrian, check out her website at bunheadwithducttape.com, or email her at lieberrian@yahoo.com.